DC COMICS
SUPER HEROES

THE WORLD OF THE SUPER HEROES

WRITTEN BY DANIEL LIPKOWITZ

CONTENTS

Bowler hat

Crowbar

THE RIDDLER

Black mask

Utility belt

BANE

Mask with cat ears

Whip

CATWOMAN

Silver coin

Orange and
purple suit

TWO-FACE

Search lights

BANK

Prison uniform

INTRODUCTION

ver the course of its initial three-year run,
he line provided enough heroes, villains and
enchmen to populate your very own brick-
uilt Gotham City – not to mention multiple
ersions of the Dark Knight himself.

The launch of the LEGO® DC Comics Super
Heroes theme in 2012 not only marked the

long-awaited return of LEGO Batman sets
but also added other iconic characters from
the DC Comics universe.

Finally, you could create your own minifigure
Justice League of America and team up to
battle Lex Luthor, the Joker and all their
chaos-causing criminal cohorts!

DATA FILE

Set Name: Batmobile and the
Two-Face Chase

Year: 2012

Set Number: 6864

Pieces: 531

DATA FILES

Throughout the book, sets are
identified with a data file (see example
left), which provides the official name
of the set, the year it was first
released, the LEGO identification
number of the set, the number of
LEGO pieces, or elements, in each set
(excluding minifigures).

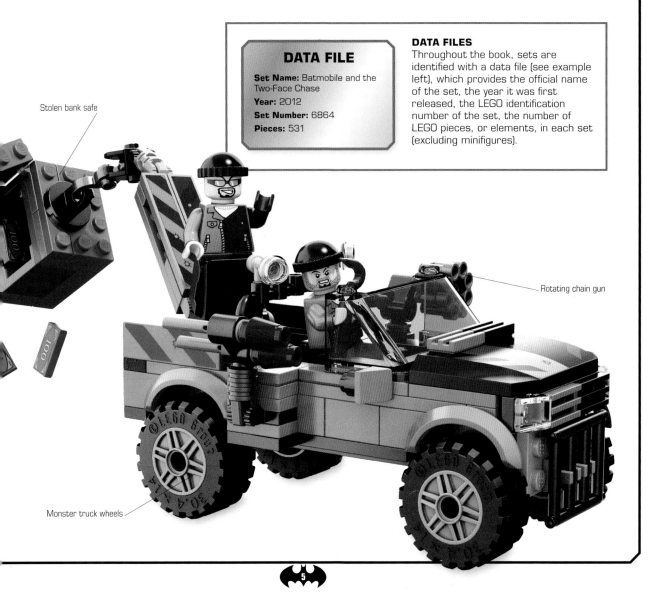

Stolen bank safe

Rotating chain gun

Monster truck wheels

BATMAN (2012)

THE NEW LEGO® DC Universe™ Super Heroes theme has expanded to include the entire universe of DC Comics, but Batman is definitely still the star of the show. Out of all the LEGO sets in the theme's debut year, there's only one that doesn't star the Dark Knight himself. After all, nobody else has the variety of equipment, vehicles and building potential of Batman!

Translucent rocket trail doubles as support stand

Jet booster core

▶ Batman Jetpack

When the mission calls for speed over size, Batman straps on his bat-winged jetpack and takes to the skies. With a new plastic wing element that replaces his familiar cape and a rocket booster in back, Batman is all set to chase down Catwoman and put a stop to her latest jewel theft.

GIVEAWAY
The first Batman minifigure in the new line is this limited-edition movie-based version, which was originally given away to lucky fans at the LEGO booth at the San Diego Comic-Con in 2011.

Batarang

Plastic glider wing-pack

Bruce Wayne (2012)

Just like in 2006, Batman's alter ego Bruce Wayne is only available in minifigure form as part of a big Batcave set. With a lighter blue suit and a much sterner expression than the original version, Bruce looks ready to don his crime-fighting gear at a moment's notice.

▼ Batsuits (2012)

The main theme includes two new Batman costume variants: a grey and blue Batsuit based on his classic comic-book look from the 1960s–1990s, and an all-black version similar to the one he started wearing in 1995. Both have removable masks and share the same double-sided head.

ROBIN RETURNS
Tim Drake adopted this red-and-black costume in honour of Superboy. His double-sided 2012 head features a smirk and a look of alarm.

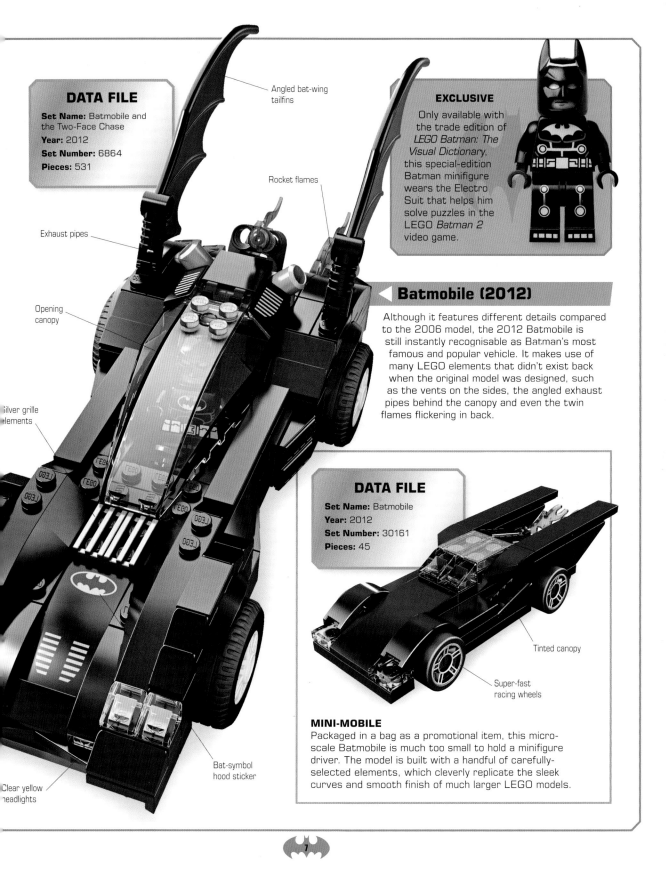

DATA FILE

Set Name: Batmobile and the Two-Face Chase
Year: 2012
Set Number: 6864
Pieces: 531

Angled bat-wing tailfins

Rocket flames

Exhaust pipes

Opening canopy

Silver grille elements

EXCLUSIVE

Only available with the trade edition of *LEGO Batman: The Visual Dictionary*, this special-edition Batman minifigure wears the Electro Suit that helps him solve puzzles in the LEGO *Batman 2* video game.

Batmobile (2012)

Although it features different details compared to the 2006 model, the 2012 Batmobile is still instantly recognisable as Batman's most famous and popular vehicle. It makes use of many LEGO elements that didn't exist back when the original model was designed, such as the vents on the sides, the angled exhaust pipes behind the canopy and even the twin flames flickering in back.

DATA FILE

Set Name: Batmobile
Year: 2012
Set Number: 30161
Pieces: 45

Tinted canopy

Super-fast racing wheels

MINI-MOBILE

Packaged in a bag as a promotional item, this micro-scale Batmobile is much too small to hold a minifigure driver. The model is built with a handful of carefully-selected elements, which cleverly replicate the sleek curves and smooth finish of much larger LEGO models.

Bat-symbol hood sticker

Clear yellow headlights

BAT-VEHICLES

THE LEGO DC Super Heroes line features many models that are familiar for fans of the original LEGO Batman theme. But, just like the Dark Knight himself, they've all been completely redesigned for a totally new building and playing experience. With different sizes, details and hidden surprises, these high-speed, high-tech vehicles are the latest tools in Batman's battle against crime!

Batwing (2012)

Smaller and more nimble than its 2006 predecessor, the new Batwing retains the original's bat-symbol shape and the split-apart wings that conceal secret weapons. Only this time, the hidden weapons are a pair of blue-tipped flick-firing missiles designed to attack aerial threats, such as the Joker's own rebuilt Joker Copter.

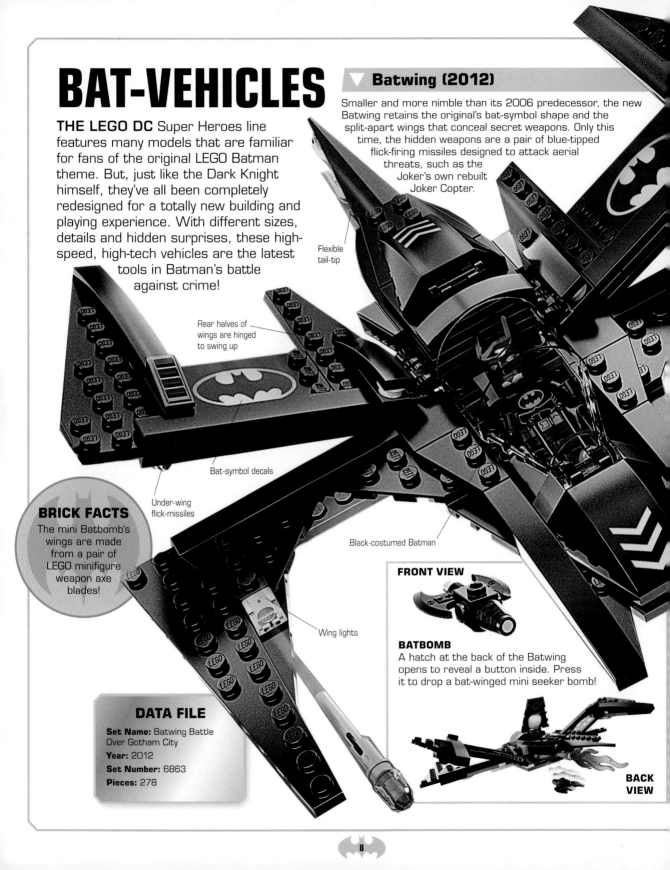

Flexible tail-tip

Rear halves of wings are hinged to swing up

Bat-symbol decals

Under-wing flick-missiles

Black-costumed Batman

Wing lights

BRICK FACTS
The mini Batbomb's wings are made from a pair of LEGO minifigure weapon axe blades!

FRONT VIEW

BATBOMB
A hatch at the back of the Batwing opens to reveal a button inside. Press it to drop a bat-winged mini seeker bomb!

BACK VIEW

DATA FILE
Set Name: Batwing Battle Over Gotham City
Year: 2012
Set Number: 6863
Pieces: 278

Adjustable handlebars

Exhaust pipes

Batcycle (I)

A well-equipped vigilante always has back-ups. In LEGO DC Super Heroes, Batman has his choice of two different Batcycles. This one, included in The Dynamic Duo Funhouse Escape set, matches Batman's blue and grey uniform and boasts sharp angles and finned exhaust pipes at the back...

DATA FILE

Set Name: The Dynamic Duo Funhouse Escape
Year: 2012
Set Number: 6857
Pieces: 380

Both tyres the same size

Batcycle (II)

...while the more curved and streamlined Batcycle from the Batcave set has a darker colour scheme, a pair of firing flick-missile launchers, and an aerodynamic shield over the front wheel to protect the engine.

DATA FILE

Set Name: The Batcave
Year: 2012
Set Number: 6860
Pieces: 690

Flick-missile

Smaller front tyre

Headlights

PURSUIT MODE

The Batwing's wings can be flattened down to create a streamlined shape for pursuit.

DATA FILE

Set Name: Bat Jetski
Year: 2012
Set Number: 30160
Pieces: 40

Movable fins

Bat Jetski

Like the mini-Batmobile, this small boat for patrolling Gotham Harbour is a special bagged promotional set. Unlike that microscale model, though, the Bat Jetski is built to minifigure scale and even comes with a Batman minifigure with a newly updated cowl piece to pilot it.

Water blasters

BATMAN™
IN
The Penguin
AND MR FREEZE'S
INVASION

THE BATCAVE

HEH HEH HEH! AT LAST WE'VE FOUND BATMAN'S SECRET LAIR!

NOT SO FAST, PENGUIN!

I'LL TAKE CARE OF HIM. YOU GO FIND BATMAN.

PENGUINS: ATTACK!

WHAM

KLANG

HA! NOTHIN GETS THROU MY ARMOUR UMBRELLA

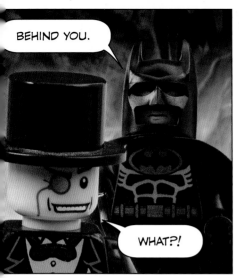

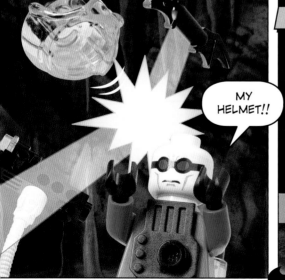

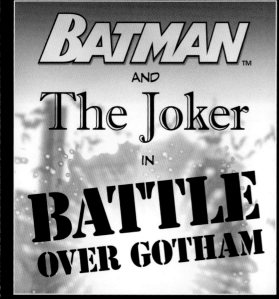

BATMAN™
AND
The Joker
IN
BATTLE
OVER GOTHAM

THE BATSIGNAL!

THE BATWING LAUNCHES INTO THE SKIES...

MEANWHILE, IN DOWNTOWN GOTHAM...

SWOOOOSH

POLICE CHANNELS ARE REPORTING AN EXPLOSION DOWNTOWN...

HEE HEE HEE! BOOM!

THOOOM!

BATCAVE II

WITH A BRAND NEW theme comes a brand new Batcave. The 2012 redesign of the Caped Crusader's subterranean lair may be a little smaller than the first one, but it adds plenty of updated features like slide-open access doors for Bat-vehicles and an inventive drop-down function that transforms Bruce Wayne into Batman. There are also new yellow and blue elements that liven up the underground atmosphere. Looks like Alfred's been redecorating!

▼ Master Control

Sorry, Robin — there's no seat for you at the control centre's high-tech Batcomputer this time. The latest upgrade to the Batcave's cutting-edge hardware features three transparent screens with angled consoles, a swivelling chair and a piping hot mug of coffee for those late nights of crime-solving.

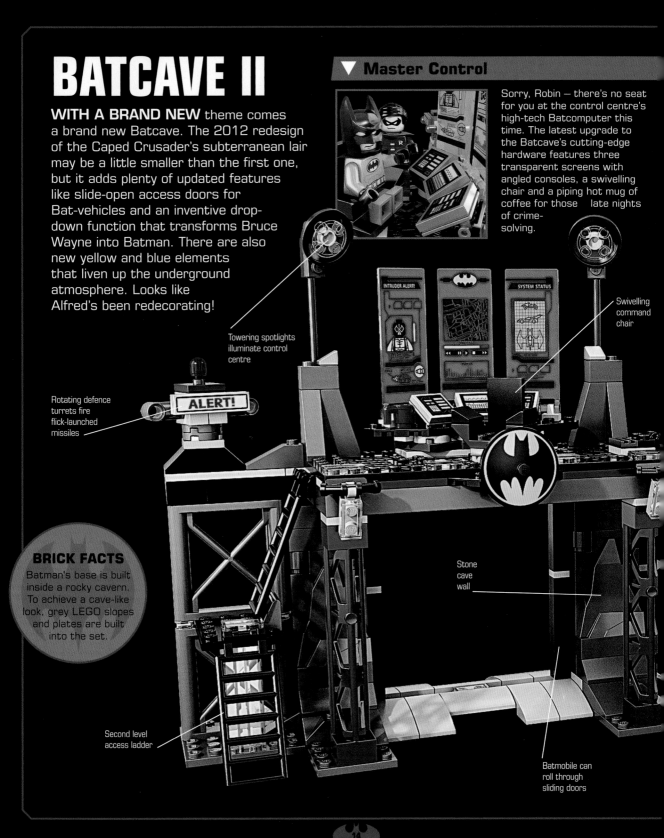

Towering spotlights illuminate control centre

Rotating defence turrets fire flick-launched missiles

ALERT!

Swivelling command chair

INTRUDER ALERT!

SYSTEM STATUS

BRICK FACTS
Batman's base is built inside a rocky cavern. To achieve a cave-like look, grey LEGO slopes and plates are built into the set.

Stone cave wall

Second level access ladder

Batmobile can roll through sliding doors

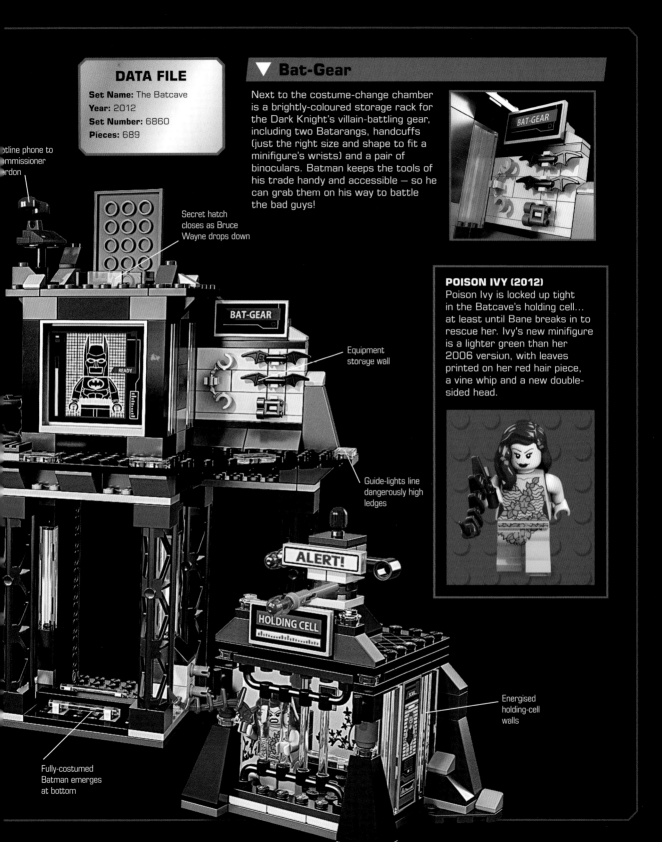

DATA FILE

Set Name: The Batcave
Year: 2012
Set Number: 6860
Pieces: 689

▼ **Bat-Gear**

Next to the costume-change chamber is a brightly-coloured storage rack for the Dark Knight's villain-battling gear, including two Batarangs, handcuffs (just the right size and shape to fit a minifigure's wrists) and a pair of binoculars. Batman keeps the tools of his trade handy and accessible — so he can grab them on his way to battle the bad guys!

otline phone to
mmissioner
rdon

Secret hatch closes as Bruce Wayne drops down

BAT-GEAR

Equipment storage wall

Guide-lights line dangerously high ledges

POISON IVY (2012)

Poison Ivy is locked up tight in the Batcave's holding cell… at least until Bane breaks in to rescue her. Ivy's new minifigure is a lighter green than her 2006 version, with leaves printed on her red hair piece, a vine whip and a new double-sided head.

Energised holding-cell walls

ALERT!

HOLDING CELL

Fully-costumed Batman emerges at bottom

DC HEROES & VILLAINS

THE LEGO DC Super Heroes theme opens up an entire world of LEGO construction beyond the borders of Gotham City. Finally, Batman can join forces with some of his most famous friends and teammates from the world of DC Comics, now captured in minifigure form for the very first time — and together they can battle a host of terrifying super-villains!

▼ Superman

Rocketed to Earth as a baby to escape his home planet's destruction, Kal-El gained incredible strength, flight and vision powers. Now he lives a double life in the city of Metropolis as mild-mannered reporter Clark Kent and Superman, the world's most powerful super hero. His minifigure has two face prints: one serious and one with a cheeky grin.

Original hairpiece with iconic S-curl

Symbol of Kryptonian heritage

Classic costume with red cape

▼ Wonder Woman

Diana is a warrior princess from the Amazon island of Themyscira. She uses her powers of super-strength, speed, agility and flight to fight for peace and justice as Wonder Woman. In minifigure form, she has a unique hairpiece with a painted tiara and her head piece features both smiling and battle-ready faces. Wonder Woman's magical Golden Lasso of Truth compels anyone it catches to speak only the truth. Made of flexible plastic, this accessory can fit around other minifigures to capture them.

Lasso of Truth

Unique hairpiece with painted tiara

Elaborate costume print

BRICK FACTS
Superman was first available as a giveaway at New York Comic-Con in October 2011, with a card promoting the LEGO Super Heroes Unite! contest.

KRYPTONITE
Superman's greatest vulnerability is to Kryptonite, a glowing crystal created by the explosion of his home world of Krypton. In its most common green form, Kryptonite weakens Superman and removes his powers, which makes it highly prized by the bad guys. Other varieties like red and gold Kryptonite have additional strange and dangerous effects.

Translucent green LEGO crystal

GREEN LANTERN
Based on his movie costume, this minifigure of Hal Jordan, the power ring-wielding hero Green Lantern, was exclusively released as a giveaway at San Diego Comic-Con and New York Comic-Con in 2011.

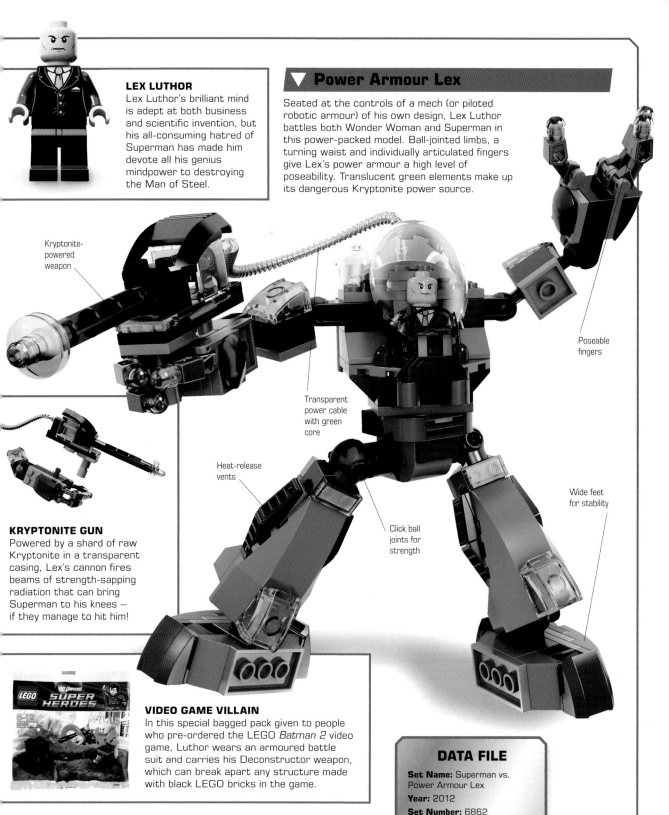

LEX LUTHOR

Lex Luthor's brilliant mind is adept at both business and scientific invention, but his all-consuming hatred of Superman has made him devote all his genius mindpower to destroying the Man of Steel.

▼ Power Armour Lex

Seated at the controls of a mech (or piloted robotic armour) of his own design, Lex Luthor battles both Wonder Woman and Superman in this power-packed model. Ball-jointed limbs, a turning waist and individually articulated fingers give Lex's power armour a high level of poseability. Translucent green elements make up its dangerous Kryptonite power source.

Kryptonite-powered weapon

Poseable fingers

Transparent power cable with green core

Heat-release vents

Click ball joints for strength

Wide feet for stability

KRYPTONITE GUN

Powered by a shard of raw Kryptonite in a transparent casing, Lex's cannon fires beams of strength-sapping radiation that can bring Superman to his knees — if they manage to hit him!

VIDEO GAME VILLAIN

In this special bagged pack given to people who pre-ordered the LEGO *Batman 2* video game, Luthor wears an armoured battle suit and carries his Deconstructor weapon, which can break apart any structure made with black LEGO bricks in the game.

DATA FILE

Set Name: Superman vs. Power Armour Lex
Year: 2012
Set Number: 6862
Pieces: 207

THE JOKER

WHEN BATMAN returned for LEGO DC Universe Super Heroes, it was obvious that his arch-enemy couldn't be far behind. In fact, as the lone villain to make appearances in multiple sets in the first year of releases, the Joker is tied with Robin the Boy Wonder as the second most prolific minifigure in the theme — a fact that probably drives the Joker batty!

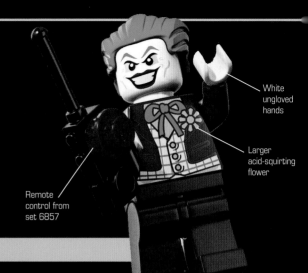

White ungloved hands

Larger acid-squirting flower

Remote control from set 6857

▶ The Joker (2012)

The Clown Prince of Crime is back, and he's just as mercilessly mirthful as ever. The new Joker retains his classic purple suit, but with the addition of a chequered green waistcoat and lots of extra detail on the front and back of his torso. He sports a different hairstyle and has two new faces: a sarcastic smirk and his trademark toothy grin.

CRANKY CLOWN
The Joker is aided and abetted in his antisocial antics by a brand-new henchman who looks pretty grumpy despite his clown makeup. The Joker's name and face are printed on the back of his jacket.

Custom "J" tailfin

Spinning rotor blades

◀ The Joker Copter (2012)

Along with the new Joker comes an all-new Joker Copter. This one has three rotor blades, a quartet of flick-firing missiles and a Joker-faced "toxic laughing gas" bomb with a big orange clown nose that fires out the front when you slam a button in the back.
There's also a ladder for the Joker to hang off and wave his new prank gun around.

DATA FILE
Set Name: Batwing Battle Over Gotham City
Year: 2012
Set Number: 6863
Pieces: 278

Joker-face logo

Rope ladder

Laughing gas bomb

CATWOMAN

CATWOMAN STRIKES again! It may be six years later, but Gotham City's most talented cat burglar is still up to the same old tricks. Along with her Catcycle, Catwoman's second set includes a buildable Gotham street corner complete with mailbox, traffic light, newspaper stand and a pile of boxes — perfect props for Batman to demolish with his Batarang as he tries to prevent Catwoman's speedy getaway.

DATA FILE

Set Name: Catwoman Catcycle City Chase
Year: 2012
Set Number: 6858
Pieces: 89

Stolen diamond

Headlight

Whip storage clip

Flip-down bike stands

▶ Catcycle (2012)

Catwoman's sleek new motorbike shares the basic construction and colour scheme of the original LEGO model, but different details give it a slightly less cartoonish cat-like design. Gone are the obvious eyes and ears, and the back now looks like it has a long black tail with a brake-light at the end.

BRICK FACTS
Catwoman's mask may look like the same one she came with in 2006, but it's actually a new piece with closer-together eye holes!

Three-way traffic light

Mailbox

▲ Gotham Street Corner

This section of Gotham City sidewalk isn't just for decoration. The traffic light at the top of the tall pole is held in place by a hook made from a minifigure wrench accessory, making it easy to knock down onto Catwoman's bike — or the Dark Knight's head if you'd prefer to let her escape with the loot this time!

▼ Catwoman (2012)

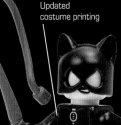

Updated costume printing

Catwoman's second minifigure is based on the same costume as her first one, but with a completely new torso print. Her new design continues on the back of her torso and her old rope belt has been replaced with a new, trendier version.

CAT'S FACE
Catwoman now wears purple lipstick, has blue goggles instead of silver and bears a wicked expression on both of her faces.

Stolen bank safe

Articulated crane arm

Flick-fire missile launcher

TWO-FACE

TWO-FACE IS BACK, and that means twice the trouble for Batman and the good citizens of Gotham City. This villain may have a whole new style, but he is still of two minds about everything — including whether he should drive off with his boosted bank safe, or just blow it open on the spot!

DATA FILE

Set Name: Batmobile and the Two-Face Chase
Year: 2012
Set Number: 6864
Pieces: 531

Rotating cannon

New silver coin with printed decoration

Reinforced prison-bar bumper

▶ Two-Face (2012)

Harvey Dent has dropped his old look for an outfit based on his very first comic book appearance in 1942. Decked out in an orange and purple suit, with an updated face print, his 2012 minifigure really stands out from the crowd.

▲ Two-Face's Tow Truck

Two-Face's ride is just as divided as its owner. A combination of brightly-coloured bricks and warning-stripe stickers decorate this beefed-up tow truck with a half-orange, half-purple theme — right down to the swivelling and jointed crane arm in back. In keeping with Two-Face's split personality, each side of the truck is armed with a different weapon.

DOUBLE TROUBLE
This time around, Two-Face has the help of a pair of henchmen in matching two-toned jackets. Although he often works with twins, these guys don't seem to be related.

HENCHMAN #1

HENCHMAN #2

BANK

Blast-out window

Teller booth

Opening door

◀ Gotham City Bank

What's a bank robbery action scene without a bank? This bank section features a teller window and computer, a safe stuffed with hundred-dollar bills and a big double-window that "explodes" out with the twist of a lever. The bank guard has a walkie-talkie and handcuffs... but will that be enough to stop Two-Face?

BANK GUARD 2012

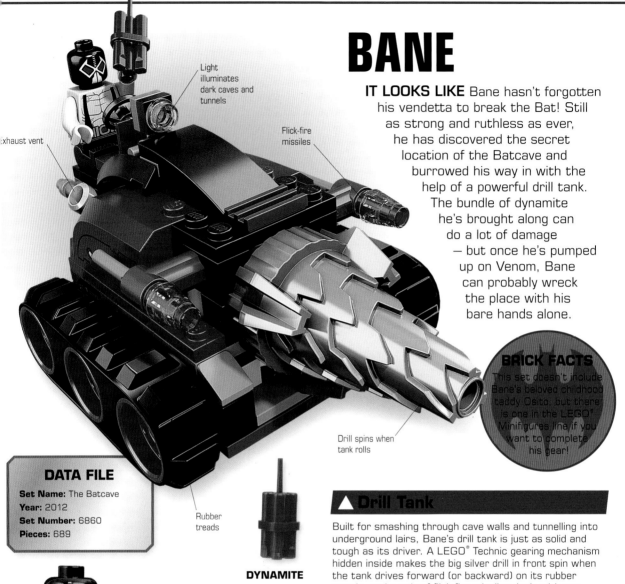

BANE

IT LOOKS LIKE Bane hasn't forgotten his vendetta to break the Bat! Still as strong and ruthless as ever, he has discovered the secret location of the Batcave and burrowed his way in with the help of a powerful drill tank. The bundle of dynamite he's brought along can do a lot of damage — but once he's pumped up on Venom, Bane can probably wreck the place with his bare hands alone.

Light illuminates dark caves and tunnels

Flick-fire missiles

Exhaust vent

Drill spins when tank rolls

BRICK FACTS
This set doesn't include Bane's beloved childhood teddy Osito, but there is one in the LEGO® Minifigures line if you want to complete his gear!

DATA FILE
Set Name: The Batcave
Year: 2012
Set Number: 6860
Pieces: 689

Rubber treads

DYNAMITE

▲ Drill Tank

Built for smashing through cave walls and tunnelling into underground lairs, Bane's drill tank is just as solid and tough as its driver. A LEGO® Technic gearing mechanism hidden inside makes the big silver drill in front spin when the tank drives forward (or backward) on its rubber treads, and a pair of flick-fire missiles deals with any walls or vehicles that get in the way.

◀ Bane (2012)

Although Bane wears the same costume as in 2006 (and throughout his comic book appearances since his introduction in 1993), his minifigure now wears a black suit instead of blue. His mask and torso details have also been redesigned with a more prominent zip on his forehead and a red buckle on his belt. He's got more defined muscles, and he's taken his gloves off, too — looks like he means business!

BACK OF THE PACK
The printing on the reverse of Bane's torso has changed as well. His Venom dispenser tube now curves around more and plugs into the back of his mask at a single central point.

THE FUNHOUSE

WHY SHOULD BATMAN be the only one with a secret headquarters? The Joker and the Riddler have joined forces to build their own booby-trapped Funhouse to challenge the wits and reflexes of the Dynamic Duo, and they've even brought Harley Quinn along for the ride. Batman and Robin are about to discover that it's not all fun and games at this crazy carnival!

Cane is a crowbar piece

Rare purple hands

◄ The Riddler (2012)

The Joker may have a wild imagination, but the Riddler is definitely the brains behind the Funhouse. He has even installed a riddle-dispensing replica of his head to tease the heroes with tricky trivia. The Riddler's new minifigure has a redesigned, more muscular torso and a belt, a bowler hat and a question-mark cane.

◄ In Jest

No one ever accused the Joker of being humble — his grinning face is plastered all over the Funhouse! It's not the only expression his 2012 minifigure is capable of, though. Flip his face around and it's a whole new look for the Dark Knight's laughing nemesis.

DATA FILE
Set Name: The Dynamic Duo Funhouse Escape
Year: 2012
Set Number: 6857
Pieces: 380

Coaster rails

Trivia booth, featuring a riddle-asking Riddler's head

Car smashes through Joker-face gate

▲ House of Fun

Each of the villains gets his or her own section of the Funhouse to play in. The Riddler has a hidden trap door, Harley Quinn has a rocking floor panel and a giant hammer to send Batman flying and the Joker rules the heights with a remote-control crane to dangle the captured Teen Wonder over a barrel of toxic doom... and fish.

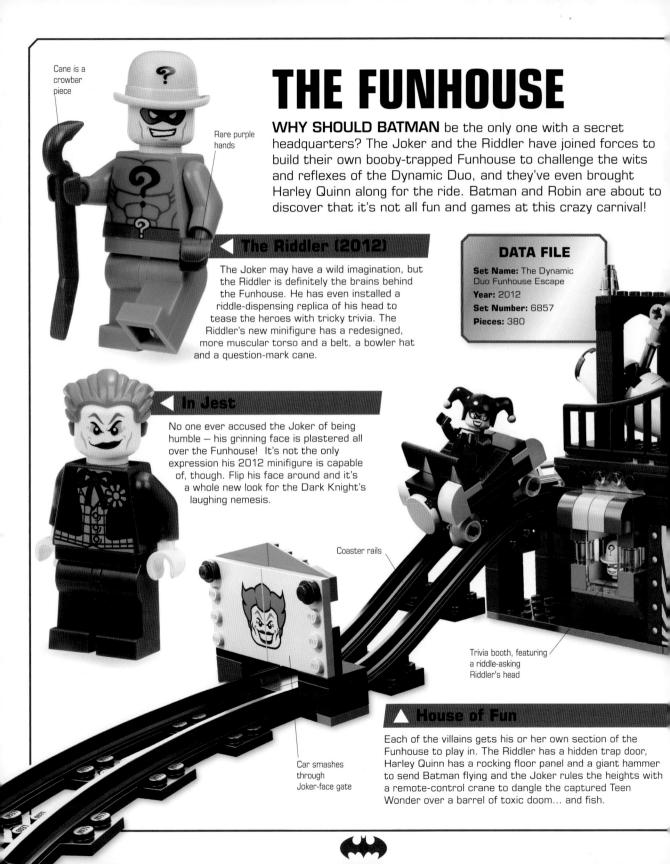

Sign tells everybody who's in charge

Turn wheel to lower the rope

Hero-smacking hammer

Trick floor plate rocks from side to side

▼ Harley Quinn (2012)

The second version of Harley Quinn is similar to the first, but with an updated torso print featuring a pointier clown collar and two new expressions: a mischievous smirk and a smile to match Mister J's. Her runaway roller coaster car is part of a trap for Batman, but she's just as likely to ride it herself for fun.

Colours match Harley's costume

Translucent carnival lights

Barrel full of Joker Venom

Sinister staircase

BRICK FACTS
Most of the LEGO DC Universe Super Heroes models, including this one, come with a comic book telling that set's story!

LEGO® ULTRABUILD

TALLER THAN a minifigure! Quicker to build than a Batmobile! It's LEGO® Ultrabuild! Launched alongside the first series of LEGO DC Universe Super Heroes sets in 2012, these big, chunky "constraction" (a combination of construction and action) figures use a ball-joint assembly system and clip-on armour plates to make bigger, ultra-poseable, powered-up heroes and villains.

DATA FILE

Set Name: Batman
Year: 2012
Set Number: 4526
Pieces: 40

▼ The Joker

The wildly unpredictable Joker lives up to his reputation... who would have guessed his Ultrabuild figure would have more pieces than any character on this page? The Ultrabuild Joker may lack the broad shoulders of the good guys, but he makes up for it with his spiked power suit and translucent blaster.

Maniacal grin

"Shocking" electro-tie

Curved coat-tail spikes

Brightly-coloured costume

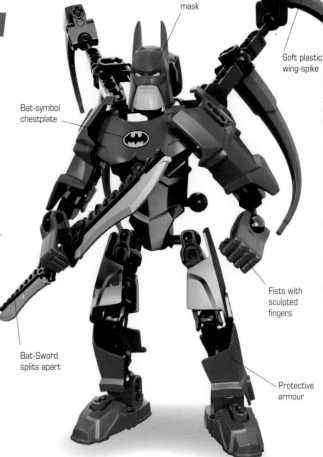

Non-removable mask

Soft plastic wing-spike

Bat-symbol chestplate

Fists with sculpted fingers

Bat-Sword splits apart

Protective armour

DATA FILE

Set Name: The Joker
Year: 2012
Set Number: 4527
Pieces: 57

▲ Batman

Never one to be left behind by a new technology, the Dark Knight has upgraded his armour to face the Joker. Along with converting his cape into a set of spiky wings, he's replaced his usual Batarang with a giant double-bladed Bat-Sword. Each ball-joint on the Ultrabuild figures can hold many different positions, making the characters extremely poseable.

▼ Green Lantern

The first non-Bat character to get an Ultrabuild set, Green Lantern is based on Hal Jordan's classic costume from the comics. Green Lantern's power ring lets him project constructs of solid energy, with their shapes defined by his imagination and the strength of his willpower. The set represents one of these constructs with a clear green spiked mace with a spinning tip.

DATA FILE
Set Name: Green Lantern
Year: 2012
Set Number: 4528
Pieces: 38

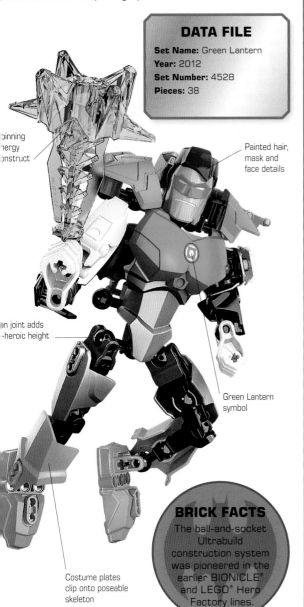

Spinning energy construct

Painted hair, mask and face details

Con joint adds -heroic height

Green Lantern symbol

Costume plates clip onto poseable skeleton

BRICK FACTS
The ball-and-socket Ultrabuild construction system was pioneered in the earlier BIONICLE® and LEGO® Hero Factory lines.

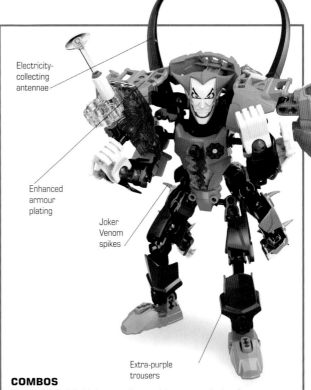

Electricity-collecting antennae

Enhanced armour plating

Joker Venom spikes

Extra-purple trousers

COMBOS
The LEGO DC Universe Super Heroes website features downloadable instructions for alternative builds and "combi" versions. These upgrade an Ultrabuild figure with extra parts taken from a second figure, which combine to create a more powerful version of the character.

Yellow and orange constructs — Green Lantern must be collecting more power rings!

Advanced Oan armour for extreme conditions

Penguin
Random
House

Project Editor Victoria Taylor
Editors Emma Grange, Matt Jones, Ellie Barton,
Clare Millar, Rosie Peet
Senior Designers Lisa Sodeau, David McDonald,
Mark Penfound
Designers Jon Hall, Stefan Georgiou
Additional Designers Lisa Robb, Anne Sharples
Pre-Production Producer Kavita Varma
Senior Producer Lloyd Robertson
Managing Editor Paula Regan
Design Manager Guy Harvey
Creative Manager Sarah Harland
Art Director Lisa Lanzarini
Publisher Julie Ferris
Publishing Director Simon Beecroft
Photography by Andy Crawford, Daniel Lipkowitz,
Tina Nielsen and Gary Ombler

First published in Great Britain in 2016
by Dorling Kindersley Limited
80 Strand, London, WC2R 0RL

001–298875–Jul/16

Contains content previously published in LEGO® Batman™:
Visual Dictionary (2012)

Page design copyright © 2016 Dorling Kindersley Limited
A Penguin Random House Company

A CIP catalogue record for this book
is available from the British Library.

ISBN: 978-0-2412-9291-4

Printed and bound in China

www.LEGO.com
www.dk.com

A WORLD OF IDEAS:
SEE ALL THERE IS TO KNOW

Acknowledgements
The publisher would like to thank Benjamin
Harper from Warner Bros. Consumer
Products; Corinna Van Delden, Randi
Sørensen, Michael Sørensen and Joakim
Kørner Nielsen at the LEGO Group; Sam
Delaney, Matt Ellison, Phillip Ring and
Jonathan Smith at TT Games for
supplying invaluable images and
information about the video game; Daniel
Lipkowitz for his research and writing;
Andy Crawford, Gary Ombler and Tina
Nielsen for their photography; Shari Last
and Jo Casey for editorial support;
and Satvir Sihota for design support.